CAUTION
QUAKE
DAMAGE

HURRICANE
EVACUATION
ROUTE

"LOBSTER LEARNERS" SERIES

# OUR POWERFUL PLANET

## The Curious Kid's Guide to Tornadoes, Earthquakes, and Other Phenomena

written by
Tim O'Shei

Lobster Press™

*To all the young scientists who care about our powerful planet*
*and want to make it a better place. – Tim O'Shei*

Our Powerful Planet: The Curious Kid's Guide to Tornadoes, Earthquakes, and Other Phenomena
Text © 2008 Tim O'Shei

Published by Lobster Press™
1620 Sherbrooke Street West, Suites C & D
Montréal, Québec   H3H 1C9
Tel. (514) 904-1100 • Fax (514) 904-1101 • www.lobsterpress.com

Publisher: Alison Fripp
Editor: Meghan Nolan
Editorial Assistants: Emma Stephen & Brynn Smith-Raska
Illustrations: Karl Edwards
Graphic Design & Production: Tammy Desnoyers


Library and Archives Canada Cataloguing in Publication

O'Shei, Tim
        Our powerful planet : the curious kid's guide to tornadoes, earthquakes, and other phenomena / Tim O'Shei ;
Karl Edwards, illustrator.

(Lobster learners series)
ISBN 978-1-897073-91-9

        1. Natural disasters--Juvenile literature.  I. Edwards, Karl II. Title.

GB5019.082 2008                     j904'.5                     C2008-901077-9

**Front Cover:** *From top, moving clockwise:* tornado, tsunami, snow-covered mountains, lightning over a field, hurricane winds, hurricane Dennis (2005/NASA), volcano eruption; middle photo: drought-cracked earth.

**Back Cover:** *Top left:* lightning bolts; *Top right:* lava.

**Front Endsheets:** *Top row, moving left to right:* hurricane Douglas (2002/NASA), drought-cracked earth (© University Corporation for Atmospheric Research/Carlye Calvin), tornado (© University Corporation for Atmospheric Research/Eugene McCaul), wildfire, Wasatch Fault (Utah Geological Survey); *Second row, left to right:* crops devastated by hailstorm, tornado (© University Corporation for Atmospheric Research), lightning bolt, clouds at sunset (FEMA/Bill Koplitz), ice-covered thistle (© University Corporation for Atmospheric Research/Carlye Calvin), earthquake warning sign, snowstorm (© University Corporation for Atmospheric Research/Bob Henson); *Third row, left to right:* mature cumulonimbus cloud (© University Corporation for Atmospheric Research), volcanic eruption, flood (FEMA/Bob McMillan), storm at sea, avalanche rescue dog (FEMA/Andrea Booher), black ice on pavement; *Bottom row, left to right:* view above the clouds, sleet pellets close-up, cirrus clouds, Mt. Erebus (Philip R. Kyle), ice storm damage, hurricane evacuation sign, sunrise from Mt. Sinai (© University Corporation for Atmospheric Research/Caspar Ammann).

**Back Endsheets:** *Top row, moving left to right:* rainbow (© University Corporation for Atmospheric Research/Bob Henson); flood warning, cumulus clouds over a lake, snow-covered mountains, Lascar volcano eruption (© University Corporation for Atmospheric Research/Caspar Ammann); aurora borealis (northern lights); *Second row, left to right:* Mt. Santiaguito (© University Corporation for Atmospheric Research/Richard Cadle), clouds over the ocean at sunrise (© University Corporation for Atmospheric Research), hurricane Katrina aftermath, hurricane Erin (2001/NASA); tornado damage (© University Corporation for Atmospheric Research), cumulonimbus cloud over a field (© University Corporation for Atmospheric Research); *Third row, left to right:* view of a storm from the beach, rime ice close-up (© University Corporation for Atmospheric Research), lighting storm over a city, tornado (© University Corporation for Atmospheric Research/Harald Richter), aurora borealis (© University Corporation for Atmospheric Research), winter conditions warning (FEMA/Marvin Nauman), lightning bolt; *Bottom row, left to right:* flooded street (FEMA/Marty Bahamond), volcano, raindrops close-up, magma close-up, crashing waves (© University Corporation for Atmospheric Research/Carlye Calvin).

Printed and bound in Singapore.

# TABLE OF CONTENTS

# LEGEND

Throughout the book, you'll come across the following:

*Did You Know?*
Surprising facts about what happens on our powerful planet.

*Phenomenal Facts*
Unbelievable-but-true info about Earth and beyond.

*Global Warming*
The Earth is getting warmer ... and this changes the phenomena that happen on our planet. Find out what's going on in the air, on the ground, and in the water that affects – or is affected by – global warming, also commonly known as "climate change."

*Power Punch*
Get the scoop on how strong our planet's phenomena can be.

## Question: What on Earth is happening? Answer: *A lot.*

Consider this: right now, as many as 1,800 thunderstorms are raging around Earth. By the time you finish reading this sentence, 500 lightning bolts will have flashed around the planet. Somewhere on Earth, a volcano is oozing lava so hot that if you threw in a penny for good luck, the coin would instantly melt into nothing. Earth is a powerful planet – and a noisy one, too. Have you ever heard a freight train rumble by? A roaring tornado sounds the same. Have you ever heard the Earth humming? Probably not, but it does – too quietly for the human ear to detect without special equipment. Earth is a changing planet, too. It's getting warmer, and though you probably haven't noticed it, our planet has.

The seemingly magical things like this that happen on and around Earth are often called phenomena. To scientists, a phenomenon is an interesting event that can be explained with facts. A *meteorologist* can explain why lightning strikes. A *volcanologist* can explain where lava comes from – and why it's so hot. A *seismologist* can explain why Earth sometimes shakes. In other words, it's not magic – it's science! In this book we'll investigate the science behind different air, land, and water phenomena.

You may discover things you never knew about what happens in the sky, on the ground, and under water. Scientists, too, are always making new discoveries about our planet. For example, just a few years after scientists figured out that the Earth's humming sound is made by the ocean waves, they discovered another hum – and they're trying to figure out what causes it. They're also learning more and more about the effects global warming will have on our environment. In some cases, you'll learn how global warming may be influencing these phenomena.

*Meteorologist Aaron Mentkowski studies the atmosphere and its phenomena.* Courtesy WKBW-TV, Buffalo ▼

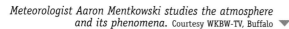

Before we begin looking at exactly what on Earth is happening and why, let's get a better understanding of how the *weather* of a place sets the stage for the air phenomena that can happen there.

Ready? Let's go for it!

## Beneath it All: The Earth's Climate

**Did You Know?** Earth has 12 different types of climates, and each of them makes it more likely that certain phenomena – particularly those that happen in the air, including thunderstorms, tornadoes, and blizzards – will happen. Among our planet's seven continents, North America is the only one to have every type of climate.

Think about the place where you live. How would you describe the weather in the spring? Summer? Winter? Autumn? And what spectacular weather events (things we'd call "phenomena") happen where you live?

The year-round weather of a place, including all four seasons, is called *climate*. How warm or cool the air is, called *temperature*, is one part of climate. Another is the amount and type of *precipitation*, mainly rain and snow. Climatic conditions depend on the temperature of the air from season to season and the amount of moisture that is in the air. These same factors make certain phenomena more likely to happen in certain places.

For example, the southeastern United States has a "humid subtropical" climate that is warm and wet year-round. Thunderstorms are fueled by hot, moist air (as you'll learn on pp. 8-9). That means thunderstorms are likely to happen all year in places like Florida, but especially in summer when the temperature is hottest.

On the other hand, while thunderstorms will also strike the northeastern Canadian city of Montreal in the summer, they're very rare (but not impossible) in winter. Montreal, unlike anywhere in Florida, has cool autumns and cold winters with plenty of snow. This makes ice storms and blizzards much more likely than thunderstorms.

While climate makes it possible for certain phenomena to happen in different places on our planet, it isn't created by Earthly forces alone. No, climate starts with a little help from something way, way, far away in outer space ... (Can you guess what it is? Turn the page to find out!)

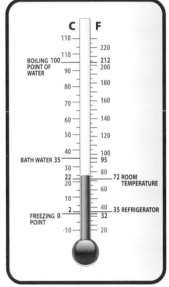

*This thermometer shows the temperature of everyday things. "C" stands for **Celsius**, which is used in most parts of the world, including Canada. "F" is for **Fahrenheit**, used in the United States.*

**Power Punch**
• The highest temperature ever recorded was in Africa's Sahara desert: 136° F (58° C). This heat would melt butter in minutes!
• The lowest temperature ever recorded was in Antarctica: 129° F (-89° C). This cold could freeze water in seconds!

# Our Atmosphere: The Earth's Blanket

The sun is one *hot*-tempered neighbor to Earth ... really hot at 11,000° F (6,000° C)! It's an important one, too, because the sun's rays heat our planet. However, those same rays also help create the climatic conditions that make the often-destructive air phenomena possible.

A tiny bit of the sun's heat reaches Earth, which spreads the warmth with the help of the atmosphere, a blanket of air that wraps around the planet. The sun and the atmosphere combine to heat Earth and form weather. Here's how: The sun's rays hit Earth most directly on the **equator**. (The rest of the Earth receives heat rays too, but not as intensely.) Some of the heat is absorbed by the soil, plants, and ocean water, and some of it rises back up into the atmosphere. This rising, warm air is called a low-pressure system. Once it hits the top of the troposphere (see diagram below, right) it starts moving away from the equator, growing cold and dropping. This sinking mass of cold air is called a high-pressure system. Air from high-pressure systems tends to rush toward low-pressure systems, creating wind. This always-rising warm air and always-sinking cold air moves around the Earth in big, circular patterns called convection cells, heating the planet and creating wind.

Now you know about heat and air. If that's all there was, we wouldn't have any weather – just a lot of wind! But there's a third element, the one that creates rain and snow and leads to thunderstorms, tornadoes, and hurricanes. That missing ingredient is water.

## Global Warming

▲ *Some of the sun's heat escapes from Earth and goes back into outer space. If it didn't, our temperature on a sunny day would reach as high as the temperature of the moon: 230° F (110° C).*

*At that temperature, lakes and rivers would boil. But there's a problem: Earth is the hottest it's been in 400 years. Not enough of the sun's heat is escaping back into space. As a result, Earth is getting warmer. The main reason is a gas called carbon dioxide ($CO_2$ for short), which traps more heat in the atmosphere.*

*The Earth is pretty gassy! Cars, trucks, and factories all release $CO_2$ into the air. We do too, when we breathe. Trees and other plants absorb $CO_2$, but entire forests are being cut down for wood. So, Earth has fewer trees on the ground and more $CO_2$ in air. As a result, scientists predict that our planet's temperature will rise 3°-7° F by 2100.*

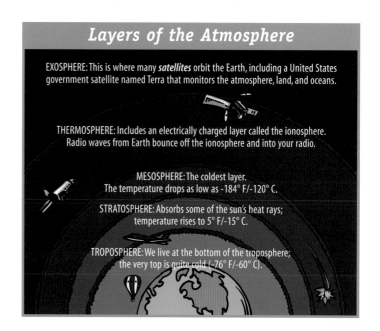

## Layers of the Atmosphere

**EXOSPHERE:** This is where many *satellites* orbit the Earth, including a United States government satellite named Terra that monitors the atmosphere, land, and oceans.

**THERMOSPHERE:** Includes an electrically charged layer called the ionosphere. Radio waves from Earth bounce off the ionosphere and into your radio.

**MESOSPHERE:** The coldest layer. The temperature drops as low as -184° F/-120° C.

**STRATOSPHERE:** Absorbs some of the sun's heat rays; temperature rises to 5° F/-15° C.

**TROPOSPHERE:** We live at the bottom of the troposphere; the very top is quite cold (-76° F/-60° C).

# The Cycle of Rain & Snow

Water is found all over the Earth's surface, from oceans to lakes to rivers to puddles to raindrops on a tree leaf. When warm air starts rising, it carries some of this water with it in an invisible gas form called water vapor. You can't see this water – it's broken into tiny pieces spread far apart. This process is called evaporation.

As this warm, moist air rises, it mixes with the sinking, cold air in the atmosphere. This causes the water vapor to squeeze closer together and form clouds. Most clouds form about seven miles (11 km) above Earth. These clouds are actually liquid, but the water is still spread so far apart that airplanes and birds won't get wet flying through them. (Imagine walking through fog on the ground – that's the same as a cloud in the sky.)

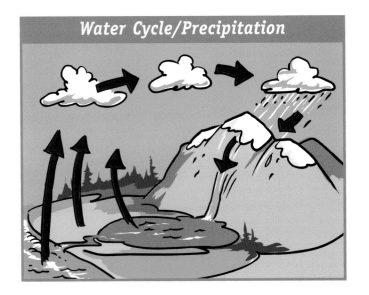

**Water Cycle/Precipitation**

Inside these clouds, cold temperatures (even in summer) form small ice crystals or even tinier particles called ice nucleators. These teeny pieces of ice collect water, making them grow into bigger raindrops or if it's cold enough, snowflakes. When the drops or flakes become heavy enough, they begin falling to Earth as precipitation. If it's cold on the ground, a snowflake will remain as snow, but in warmer weather, it will melt and become rain. Either way, the trip can be long and slow: If you could drive a car from the typical cloud to Earth, it would take seven minutes. But raindrops travel more at the speed of a bicycle. A typical raindrop falls for about an hour before reaching Earth.

Warm, moist air that holds evaporated water clashes with cold air and leads to clouds. Under certain conditions, clouds can lead to powerful storms – which is where we're headed next.

# THUNDERSTORMS: Earth's Constant Boom

It's a hot, sticky day. The air feels thick and humid. You know what that means: This warm air, full of evaporating water, will rise into the sky and slam into a mass of sinking, cold air. This air "crash" will create clouds, and the mix of high pressure and low pressure will create wind.

As the cold air sinks, it becomes warmer and warmer until it hits Earth's surface as hot air. It sweeps up more water vapor and rises high until it crashes with a new cold mass. A circular cycle is created. Remember what it's called? A convection cell. The rising air in the cell grows hotter and stronger as it moves faster and faster. Soon, this "updraft" makes the cloud grow taller – it can grow by several miles in just minutes, shooting upward like a space shuttle.

*Cumulus clouds usually ▲ form on mild weather days.*

*Updrafts cause cumulonimbus clouds ▲ like this one to shoot high into the sky. The result? Thunderstorms.*

*Thrashing air, ice, and raindrops ▲ turn thunderstorm clouds dark.*

The cloud grows darker as the hot and cold air (and the raindrops and ice pellets) inside the cloud thrash up and down. The cloud takes on the properties of a battery and creates lightning and thunder. (You'll learn how this happens on pp. 10-11.) Meanwhile, the rain and ice bounce inside the cloud like popcorn, growing larger and larger until they get heavy enough to fall to Earth.

Normally, a thundershower lasts for an hour or less. Sometimes, though, one thundercloud (called a "single cell") will link with others and form a "supercell." These larger storms can span several – sometimes even hundreds of – miles. They often rage on for half a day.

The air inside a supercell is especially strong. The updrafts can move at 170 mph (240 kph), about the same speed as a race car. Often they start spiraling upward and form a similar spinning motion downward. This is called a mesocyclone, and it can lead to tornadoes. (You'll learn more about that on pp. 12-13.)

Meteorologists use *radar* to monitor the strength and movement of thunderstorms, which can cause all sorts of damage, from floods (see pp. 16-17) to hail (see pp. 18-19). Sometimes a line of thunderstorms will curve into a shape known as a bow echo and produce a 100-mph wind (161 kph) called a derecho (deh-RAY-cho). And even if they don't do that, thunderstorms produce a dangerous phenomenon you've certainly seen – lightning. That's where we're headed next.

## Global Warming

The warmer the air, the more easily water evaporates. This extra-moist air from global warming makes thunderstorms more likely, especially around the Gulf of Mexico and the Atlantic Ocean coastline. Some scientists say that as a result, the number of days in the United States that have the right conditions for severe thunderstorms will double by 2100. That means big eastern cities like Atlanta and New York City will be twice as likely to get slammed by thunderstorms.

*Low, wide, circular shelf clouds like this one over Miles City, Montana, can form on the front edge of a big thunderstorm system. Shelf clouds are formed when wind rushing downward from the storm lifts warm, moist air into the sky. The clouds can be as wide as 12 miles (20 km) – that's roughly equal to 16,000 people holding hands in one long line.* © University Corporation for Atmospheric Research

### Did You Know?
Not all thunderstorms produce rain. During a hot and dry **drought**, the raindrops sometimes evaporate before they hit Earth. Lightning during such dry conditions can ignite wildfires.

*Jet planes usually fly over thunderstorms, but not over supercells (above). These storms can reach 11 miles (17 km) above Earth, roughly the same altitude at which a plane would fly.*

*Scientists can use lightning to track and predict storms all over the planet. This is because lightning emits radio waves – invisible energy that flows through the air and can be detected from far away. Scientists are hoping to be able to use lighting to measure the strength of storms while the storms are still over the ocean and haven't yet caused great damage.*

**W**hat's the first thing that comes to mind when you think about thunderstorms? *ZAP! BOOM!* The lightning and thunder, right? Those two phenomena actually go together: A lightning bolt is about 50,000° F (28,000° C) – five times hotter than the sun. A bolt causes the air around it to heat to 18,000° F (10,000° C), and sometimes much more. The superheated air explodes, which is what creates the boom of thunder. You'll see lightning before hearing the thunder because light travels faster than sound. Sometimes, in fact, you'll see only the lightning – the storm may be too far away for the sound to carry.

To understand how a thundercloud creates lightning, imagine putting a battery into a flashlight. The battery has a positive (+) charge on top and a negative (-) charge on bottom. The inside of the battery is full of energy. When the battery is snapped into place, that energy flows through the flashlight and makes the light-bulb shine.

Lightning works in a similar way. Inside a thundercloud, bouncing rain and ice smash into each other. These collisions cause the electrons, or negative charges, to fall from the raindrops and ice to the bottom of the cloud. In turn, the positive charges rise to the top of the cloud. Now, the cloud is like a battery: positively charged on top, negatively charged on bottom, with lots of electric energy inside.

*One famous lightning rod is the pole atop NYC's Empire State Building. It works: The building is struck by lightning about 100 times per year and has remained undamaged. Once, it was struck eight times in 24 minutes.* ▶

## Did You Know?

Lightning tends to strike the structures that are highest in the air. In the mid-1700s Benjamin Franklin came up with the idea of using a tall, metal pole to attract lightning. His thinking was that the lighting, which would be attracted to the metal, would strike the pole instead of damaging buildings. The pole would be grounded so that the electricity would flow harmlessly into the ground, rather than into the building. His idea worked. These days, lightning rods can be seen atop skyscrapers, church steeples, statues, and even houses in the middle of wide-open fields.

A lightning bolt itself travels 50,000 feet a second, or 34,000 mph (55,000 kph). Put another way: A plane flying from Los Angeles, California, to Honolulu, Hawaii, will take more than five hours. If a lightning bolt could travel the same distance (which it can't), it would get there in four-and-a-half minutes.

Lightning strikes Earth about 6,000 times every minute.

As this thundercloud moves through the troposphere, it causes electrically charged particles to gather on the surface of Earth below. Think of batteries again: When you put more than one battery in a flashlight, you make sure the negative side of one battery is touching the positive side of another. That's because electricity flows between positive and negative. When the bottom of a cloud has a negative charge, and the ground below has a positive charge, the electricity flows – in a bolt of lightning! A stream of negatively charged particles called a "stepped leader" zaps toward the ground. Meanwhile, the positively charged area on the ground sends an upward "streamer." When the leader and the streamer meet, *zap*! Lightning flashes. The bright part that the human eye can see is actually a return stroke going back up to the sky.

Occasionally the process is reversed. When the bottom of a cloud is positive, and negative particles gather on the ground, lightning can start from Earth and reach up to the cloud. Lightning also strikes in the air when the positive side of one cloud nears the negative end of another.

Next, you'll learn about one of the most devastating phenomena that thunderstorms can cause.

A single bolt contains between 50 million to 2 billion volts of electricity. That's enough energy to light anywhere between a half million to 17 million lightbulbs.

11

# TORNADOES: Earth's Twist of Nature

### Did You Know?

Tornado strength is measured by the Fujita Scale, developed in 1973 by Theodore Fujita. The numbers are determined after examining the damage that a tornado causes. A 0-level tornado is considered the weakest, with wind 65 to 85 mph (105-137 kph). A 0 tornado will break tree branches and damage things like signs and chimneys. A 3-level tornado (winds of 136-165 mph/105-138 kph) will knock over cars and ruin houses. A level 5 tornado has winds of more than 200 mph (322 kph) and can lift houses and send cars flying through the air.

The spinning air of tornadoes sounds like a freight train – and some tornadoes are strong enough to pick one up! "Twisters," as they are often called due to their upward spinning motion, move across land like a vacuum cleaner on a rug. They suck up anything in their path, including cars and houses.

Strong tornadoes can cause massive destruction. They rip roofs from homes and blow out windows from buildings. People and animals can be swept up and killed, though some have survived.

These swirling, funnel-shaped storms get their power from the same forces that create thunderstorms and lead to lightning: the up-and-down thrashing of hot and cold air. Here's what happens: When a supercell thunderstorm grows so strong that a swirling mesocyclone forms inside it, tornadoes become a possibility. At this point, meteorologists who monitor these storms will issue a tornado watch or, if the storms are very likely, a tornado warning. If the updraft in the thunderstorm system is strong enough, the mesocyclone is stretched tall and thin. Air from the ground is drawn up to feed the funnel cloud, which is working its way toward Earth. When the funnel cloud touches the ground, it becomes a tornado.

*The typical U.S. tornado registers as a 1. It has winds of 73-112 mph (117-180 kph) and is about 150 ft (46 m) wide, or the same as a hallway with six or seven classrooms. It moves at about 40 mph (64 kph). That's more than twice the speed the average person can run when sprinting.*

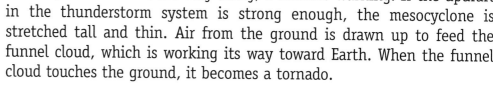

### Phenomenal Facts

Right now there is no way to control or prevent tornadoes (or any storms) from happening, but scientists are working on it. Some think that heating up thunderclouds from outer space may be the answer. Their idea is to use a **satellite** to beat hot waves (similar to the ones used in microwaves) onto a storm cloud. They think by heating up the cold rain, they'll "calm down" the cloud. By slowing or stopping the swirling winds this way, they hope to prevent tornadoes.

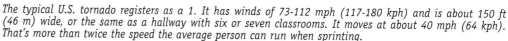

*A waterspout is a tornado that forms over water. The Florida Keys have 400-500 a year, more than anywhere else in the world. The area's hot and humid weather creates perfect conditions for waterspouts: The warm air rises, carrying evaporating water with it. The water forms clouds, and the fast-rising air starts spinning and swirling as eastward winds blow through.*

The storm follows the same path as the "mother cloud" that created it. Sometimes the tornado may even leave Earth and jump back into its mother cloud. It may disappear in there for good, or it may pop back out and continue roaring across the ground. Most tornadoes last only a few minutes until their winds slow down, but some rage on for an hour or more. One, in 1925, lasted most of a day and killed 600 people. They can get awfully big, too: A 1987 tornado in Edmonton, Alberta, had a funnel as wide as the depth of the Grand Canyon. This supersized tornado traveled 22 miles (64 km) – just a few miles short of a marathon.

▲ *A landspout is a skinny, rope-shaped tornado of whirling **condensation**. It forms when the updraft of a thunderstorm stretches circulating air upward to the storm cloud.*

Tornadoes have happened on every continent except Antarctica, which is consistently cold (tornadoes need warm air) and has calm air (tornadoes need heavy winds). The United States has more tornadoes than any other country. In fact, three-fourths of all tornadoes on Earth form in Kansas, Oklahoma, Texas, and Nebraska – an area known as "Tornado Alley." The reason these states get so many tornadoes (and thunderstorms, too) is because of the climates to the north and the south. Hot air flowing from the tropical climates of the south crashes with cold air coming from the arctic climates of the north. The flat land in "Tornado Alley" makes it especially easy for thunderstorms and tornadoes to form, since the air masses aren't slowed down by mountains.

Next you'll learn about another type of swirling storm, one that forms over water and crashes ashore like an angry monster.

### Power Punch

Tornadoes over water pick up fish and frogs. On land they pick up sand, dirt, or snow. This is why some tornadoes look dirty (soil), red (sand), or bright white (snow). Sometimes tornadoes deposit the materials they sweep up into the mother cloud. The thunderstorm cloud can carry these items for great distances and eventually send them back to Earth as rain. Frogs, clams, salamanders, and worms have all been "rained" onto the ground far from the places where they were swept up.

# HURRICANES: Earth's Swirling Storms

## Global Warming

You already know that deforestation contributes to global warming (p. 6). It also increases the chances of hurricanes causing massive damage. Thick forests slow down the heavy winds of a hurricane, which makes a forest one of the best protections against a storm. As forests are cut down for wood products, people worry that hurricanes could be even more harmful in the future.

The word hurricane comes from "Hurican," the name people who lived in the Caribbean once gave to what they believed was the god of evil. It's easy to understand why: In the Caribbean and other warm, humid places around the world, hurricanes cause death and destruction. They usually form during late summer and autumns in southern regions of the United States, plus parts of Central America, Southeast Asia, and Australia. Hurricanes start over warm ocean water (80° F/27° C) because it evaporates easily. (Some scientists point out that Earth's increasing temperature makes the ocean water warmer and, in turn, hurricanes stronger.)

*A large hurricane creates more energy than every human together on the planet uses in an entire year.*

As the warm air rises, it cools quickly in the atmosphere and forms into thunderstorms. The warm water keeps feeding the storms, and soon they grow into a large supercell. When the supercell has lasted for 24 hours, it becomes known as a "tropical disturbance." Tracking the storm from pictures taken by weather satellites that revolve around Earth, meteorologists are ready to issue a hurricane watch (if a hurricane is possible) or a warning (if it's probable). As the warm ocean water provides more and more moisture for the supercell, the storm clouds themselves begin to swirl around each other. Now this spinning mass of storms is known as a tropical depression. When the winds hit 39 mph (63 kph), the swirling system is called a tropical storm.

When the winds hit 74 mph (118 kph), or about the rate of driver who's over the speed limit on a highway, it officially becomes a hurricane – if it's in the Atlantic Ocean, that is. In the Indian Ocean, a hurricane is actually called a cyclone. And in the Pacific Ocean, it's called a typhoon.

*Storm names alternate from female to male (Arlene, Bret, Cindy, Don, etc.) and are re-used every six years. If an Atlantic hurricane causes huge amounts of damage, scientists from the World Meteorological Organization can decide to retire the name. They did this after Hurricane Katrina devastated Louisiana and Mississippi in 2005, as seen here. "Katrina" has been replaced by "Katia."*

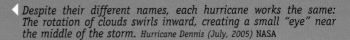

In the United States, special government planes called hurricane hunters fly above the storms and take close-up photos. Sometimes they even fly into the eye and gather the best information on the strength of the storm. This is possible because in the eye there is no wind or rain. In fact, if you were on the ground inside the eye of a hurricane, the winds would be light and the skies clear. This can trick people who are caught in a hurricane: The first part of the storm rages through, getting worse as the "eye wall" passes over. (The eye wall separates the eye from the rest of the storm, and it's where the winds and rains are heaviest.) Then, suddenly, the weather clears up. You might think the hurricane has passed. But it hasn't. As the storm system moves, the other side of the eye wall passes over, and the rest of the hurricane follows.

When a hurricane passes over land, the winds sweep up otherwise safe objects like sneakers and street signs and send them hurtling sideways like arrows shot by an archer. As with a tornado, homes and buildings are often damaged or destroyed. Heavy rains pour from the sky. **Storm surges** cause floods (see p. 16). Once a hurricane hits land and loses its warm-water power source, it begins to fade ... but not before causing a great deal of destruction and sometimes death.

Monstrous as hurricanes may be, they're not the deadliest type of weather disaster. That distinction belongs to another phenomenon – the one you'll read about next.

### Did You Know?

Hurricanes are rated on the Saffir-Simpson Hurricane Scale, which is named after Herbert Saffir, an engineer, and Robert Simpson, former director of the United States' National Hurricane Center. Saffir first developed the scale in 1971 to help design buildings that could survive hurricane-like winds. A category 1 storm is the least damaging: It has winds of up to 95 mph (153 kph) and will tear apart trees and landscaping. A category 3 hurricane has winds of 111-130 mph (178-209 kph), waves of nine to 12 feet (2.7-3.6 meters), and will seriously damage mobile homes and small buildings. A category 5 storm will cause floods several miles inland and damage most buildings. It has winds of more than 155 mph (250 kph) and waves higher than 18 feet (5.4 meters).

# FLOODS: Earth's Overflow

*Germs from garbage, sewage, and dead animals make floodwater dangerous. People who have to venture into it should keep their skin covered for protection.*

Floods cause more deaths than any other phenomenon.

A flood can start several ways: Quick, heavy cloudbursts dump rain hard and fast. If a cloudburst continued for a full hour, there would be about 5 inches (13 cm) of rain – enough to turn the ground into a small pool. Most cloudbursts are over in just minutes, but even an inch or two of rain can cause floods. Long, steady rains lead to floods, too. They soak the ground like a sponge that can't hold any more water, and they overflow rivers and streams like a bathtub with the faucet left on.

There are lots of ways floods can happen. Strong winds can cause floods by whipping up water from oceans and lakes, creating a storm surge that washes out the land. And unexpectedly warm temperatures – especially in spring – can melt snow so fast that the water floods yards. Melting chunks of ice, meanwhile, can flow downstream and clog rivers, sending waters crashing ashore.

Once flood waters surge onto open land, little can stop them. Imagine a flood that is 2 inches (5 cm) deep. That's barely enough to dip your fingers into – but it's more than enough to ruin the floor of your house. A flood of 6 inches (15 cm) – an amount that would reach just above your ankles – would knock you over if it was moving fast. Two feet (61 cm) of water wouldn't even reach the hips of the average fourth grader – but it would easily make a car float.

The shape of the land can make floods even more dangerous. In narrow canyons and valleys, floodwaters are squeezed tighter, becoming deeper and stronger and rushing faster. During a flood in Colorado in 1976, waters entered a narrow canyon and turned a small creek into one that rushed like the Mississippi River. In just minutes the water rose to 19 feet (6 m) – taller that three grown men standing on each other's shoulders. A police car floated 8 miles (13 km) downstream and was pelted by so many rocks and branches and other debris that it was nearly unrecognizable.

## Did You Know?

Areas by rivers and deep streams and creeks often have flood protection in place. Dikes and levees are long walls along a waterway meant to keep water from splashing ashore. Dams are structures in rivers meant to slow or stop the flow of water. Usually, they work – but a strong "wall of water" (as floods are often called) can break a levee, dike, or dam. In 2005 this happened in Louisiana, where waters whipped up by Hurricane Katrina broke through a levee and flooded the city of New Orleans (as seen at right).

### Global Warming

Global warming is making floods more likely. The increased temperature packs more water vapor into the atmosphere (see p. 7), which increases the amount of rain – a main cause of floods.

When ground soaks up too much water, that's a problem too – especially on the slope of a hill. The water turns well-packed dirt into loose, slippery mud. Earth's *gravity* pulls this mucky stuff downward, creating mudslides that bury homes, cars, and people.

Recovering from a flood is difficult. With nowhere to go, the water can stay for a long time.

Next you'll read about another phenomenon that makes a long-lasting impact. But instead of transforming the land into a lake, it turns it into something that resembles a skating rink. Read on!

*Driving in a flood is dangerous. Two feet (61 cm) of water will make a car float, but it takes only a half-foot (15 centimeters) to make a driver lose control or to cause a car to stall.*

*People use sandbags to protect their property from floodwaters.* ▲ *The sand acts like a dam, blocking water from flowing into places where it would cause even more damage.*

***El Niño*** *storms caused the Rio Nido mudslides in northern* ▼ *California (1993), damaging houses and cars.* FEMA/Dave Gatley

*Cities are dangerous flood spots because of all the concrete and pavement. With little soil to soak up the water, narrow alleys turn into rushing rivers, and open areas like parking lots and streets turn into lakes.*

# ICE STORMS: Earth's Deep Freeze

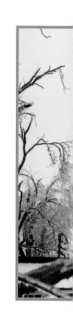

You already know the first step of an ice storm: Clouds form high in the troposphere, where temperatures drop as low as -76° F (-60° C), and ice crystals become snow. If the flakes drop to Earth and hit a mass of rising warm air, they'll melt into raindrops. This happens commonly, especially in spring and summer (and all year in warmer climates). But remember, cold air tends to sink. During winter, especially in chillier climates, there will be plenty of cold air. If these raindrops leave the warm layer and then hit air that is below the freezing mark (32° F/0° C), you won't get a rainstorm or a snowstorm … but an ice storm.

There are two main types of icy precipitation. Sleet forms when the raindrops hit a layer of cold air so thick that they have time to totally freeze before hitting Earth. When sleet falls it hits the ground, bounces around, and settles in icy piles.

The second type is freezing rain. These raindrops hit a layer of cold air that cools them but isn't quite thick enough to give them time to refreeze. Instead, this chilled rain immediately freezes on whatever it hits: tree branches, power lines, cars, streets, and so on. The ice builds up quickly. Imagine a baker pouring glaze over a cinnamon roll – the glaze will build higher and higher as it hardens on the top and sides of the dough. Freezing rain works the same way as it covers all surfaces outdoors.

*Cold climates get hit with plenty of winter storms, but the overall snowfall in North America since 1990 has been dropping. Many scientists say part of the cause is global warming: Warmer temperatures will bring more rain, less snow.*

## Power Punch

Ice storms can be crippling, but heavy snow and strong wind make for another type of nasty winter weather – blizzards. During the United States' Civil War (1861-65), the word "blizzard" was used to describe a steady stream of gunfire. Five years after the war ended, a newspaper in Indiana used the word to describe a wintry storm so windy and strong that the snow flew like bullets. Today, meteorologists still use the word to describe a snowstorm that features heavy winds – 35 mph (56 kph) or more, which is about as fast as a rabbit can run. Not only can this wind send falling snow flying sideways, but it can also whip up snow from the ground and create snowdrifts as tall as a two-story home. Blizzards create "whiteout" conditions in which you can't see more than a quarter-mile ahead.

*Hail can be the size of golf balls or larger.* ▶

▲ *Ice storms like this one can be dangerous: falling tree limbs tangle with power lines that spark and sizzle and sometimes lead to fires.*

*Two days of freezing fog formed this rime (at right). The pencil-shaped structures are pointing in the same direction as the wind blew.*
© University Corporation for Atmospheric Research (Carlye Calvin)

## Phenomenal Facts

• Warmer spring and summer days bring a different type of ice storm – hail. Hail forms when icy pellets get stuck in the choppy air of a thundercloud. The pellets bounce inside the cloud like popcorn, picking up frozen water that makes them grow larger and larger. When the hail gets big enough, it falls to the ground.

Hail is measured by the Hailstorm Intensity Scale, which runs from 0 (pea size) to 10 (volleyball size). Golf-ball-sized hail, which can break windows and kill birds, is a 4. Softball-sized hail, which damages roofs and trees, is an 8. Hail the size of volleyballs – the biggest ever in North America – fell in Aurora, Nebraska, in 2003.

• Fog in temperatures below freezing is called rime ("RHYME") or frozen fog. It freezes on contact with objects it touches. When the wind blows the rime, the ice particles build up on each other. By the end of a foggy, freezing night, a lamppost can look like a toothbrush: The lamppost is the handle, and the rime build-up looks like the brush's bristles. Rime can also freeze around falling snowflakes, creating light, icy lumps called graupel ("GRAU-puhl").

In fact, the icy build-up is called the same thing – "glaze." But this glaze isn't sweet. It takes only a quarter-inch of ice to freeze over car windshields and make roads dangerous. Meteorologists label this amount of ice a "nuisance." Between a quarter-inch and half-inch of ice – what meteorologists call "disruptive" – will make tree limbs hang low enough to pull down some power lines and cause electrical outages. Meteorologists call a half-inch of ice or more "crippling." Limbs from even the largest trees will snap and fall and tangle with power lines. Roads will be nearly impossible to travel. Think about it: all that damage comes from a layer of ice only as thick as the width of your thumb.

Ice storms – like thunderstorms, tornadoes, and hurricanes – start high above our planet and deliver a punch to the ground. The next phenomena you'll read about start deep below the Earth's surface. Let's get our heads out of the clouds and put our feet on the ground. It's time to move from air to land. Here we go!

## Earth in (Slow) Motion

The atmosphere is action packed, but the land under your feet is just as busy. Right now, do you notice that the land is moving? Probably not – but it is (very, very slowly). The Earth is made of layers, and the solid section where we live stays in constant motion by floating on a soft, molten middle section.

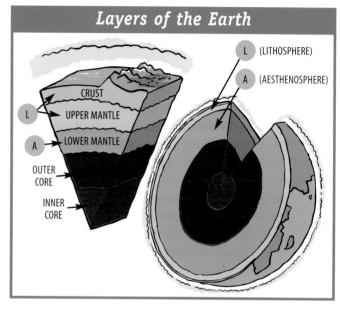

**Layers of the Earth**

L (LITHOSPHERE)

A (AESTHENOSPHERE)

CRUST

L — UPPER MANTLE

A — LOWER MANTLE

OUTER CORE

INNER CORE

If you could slice Earth in half (see diagram at right), you could see these sections. The outermost layer is called the crust. We live on top of the crust, which is made mostly of rock and soil. In many places, the crust is about 18 miles (30 km) thick, a length equal to 24,000 average-sized televisions stacked one on top of the next. That probably seems big, but compared to the rest of Earth, the crust is thin. Earth's next layer, called the mantle, is made of hot, soft rock and is about 100 times thicker than the crust – 1,800 miles (2,900 km). The thickest layer (2,200 miles/3,500 km) is the inner section, called the core. The outer part of the core is made of molten nickel and iron. The inner-most part of the core is solid iron.

To describe how this mixture of solid and liquid causes Earth's surface to move, scientists use two more words: lithosphere and aesthenosphere. The lithosphere is Earth's rocky outer portion, including all of the crust and part of the mantle. The aesthenosphere is the soft, liquid part of the lower mantle. The lithosphere is broken into more than a dozen large plates and several smaller ones. These tectonic plates actually float on the soft aesthenosphere. They're always moving – even as you read this sentence. They move about two inches (5 cm) a year, sometimes less. That's about the same rate as your fingernails grow.

*The Grand Canyon in Arizona is 277 miles (446 km) long – about three times the length of the state of Delaware. It plunges about 5,000 feet (1,520 meters) deep – slightly less than a mile. Scientists think it formed as a result of tectonic plates that moved apart and of water from what is now the Colorado River that began eroding the canyon.*

Scientists believe that more than 250 million years ago, all of Earth's land was one massive continent, which we refer to as "Pangea" (pan-JEE-uh). Over time, the land broke apart and eventually became the tectonic plates we have today. But the breakup wasn't immediate: Some scientists believe that up until 140 million years ago, five of the plates were joined together in one giant landmass called Gondwanaland. That land now forms Antarctica, Africa, Australia, South America, and India.

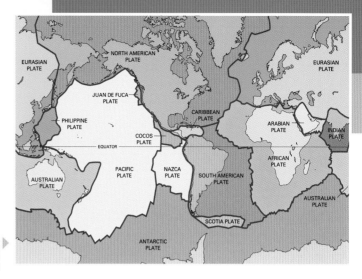

*Earth's major tectonic plates (right) are constantly moving. The plates that form North and South America are creeping west. If this continues, the Americas will eventually collide with Europe and Asia – in 350 million years.* Courtesy of USGS

Starting around 60 million years ago, this movement slowly created mountains (when plates pushed together), and canyons and oceans (when the plates pulled apart). This continues today. To see an entire mountain or canyon form, you would have to stand in the same place for millions of years. That's impossible, of course, but it's entirely possible to see (and feel) the more immediate impact of tectonic action. The movement of Earth's plates causes the next two phenomena. Turn the page and hang on tight, because we're about to enter shaky ground.

▲ *Winter weather is especially harsh high on Mount Everest (above). The average January temperature is -33° F (-36° C) and can fall as low as -76° degrees F (-60° C). Winds called jet streams that soar high in the atmosphere whack Mount Everest with the force of a hurricane.*

## Power Punch

The highest mountain range in the world, the Himalayas, was created by a high-speed collision between two plates. This "collision" actually took millions of years – but it happened much faster than usual. The plate that forms India and nearby countries is thinner and lighter than other plates. It was moving at the rate of eight inches (20 cm) a year – four times faster than most other plates. (If your fingernails grew that fast, you'd have claws within months!) When the Indian plate ran into the Asian plate, the extra speed created the Himalayas, which include the tallest mountain in the world: Mount Everest reaches higher than 29,000 feet (8,800 m) above sea level, or more than halfway to the top of the troposphere.

21

# EARTHQUAKES: Unsteady Earth

### Global Warming

Earthquakes can cause another ground-moving phenomenon – a landslide. Landslides occur when dirt and rocks (including boulders that are bigger than people) slam down the slope of a mountain, hill, or cliff. They can happen in a flash, especially when an earthquake (or volcanic eruption) loosens the ground.

Usually landslides move about as fast as a car driving at medium speed, around 30 to 50 miles per hour (48 to 80 kph). Sometimes, though, they can rush like a race car, reaching 200 miles per hour (322 kph). Global warming may make landslides more likely: Excessive rain or fast-melting snow can cause a land-slide by softening the dirt. This is especially true for snowy and icy cliffs – global warming increases the likelihood of an *avalanche*.

The constant movement of tectonic plates that you just read about causes earthquakes. By the time you finish reading this page, an earthquake will have shaken somewhere on Earth – they happen every 30 seconds. The strong ones create tremors powerful enough to break bridges and buildings. Only one in every 5,000 earthquakes causes damage. In fact, only one out of every five earthquakes can be felt. Nobody except seismologists – scientists who study tectonic plate action and the quakes that result – even notice they happened.

Seismologists closely watch places in the crust where there are faults, which are long cracks in rocky areas. When tectonic plates grind, parts of rock in the fault lines above get jammed and stuck in place – just as if you rubbed two jagged rocks together in opposite directions. The bumps and dips in each rock would make it difficult to slide the rocks smoothly. The same type of thing happens on Earth. As the plates grind, pressure builds on the jammed rocks in the fault. Eventually, when the pressure gets high enough, the rocks slip or break free. The shifting of the rocks usually happens somewhere between Earth's surface and 45 miles (72 km) deep. The jolt sends shockwaves through the crust. The most impact will be felt at the epicenter – the area on Earth's surface directly above where the rocks shifted. Most earthquakes last only a few seconds before the shockwaves fade out.

Earthquakes happen around the world, but one area sees many more than the rest. Sections of ten major tectonic plates meet in a region of the Pacific Ocean that includes Australia, Japan, and the west coasts of Canada and the United States. Four out of every five earthquakes happen in this region, which is called the "Ring of Fire." (You'll read more about it on p. 25.)

*Here, scientists monitor the Wasatch Fault, which runs 200 miles through Utah and into Idaho. It causes hundreds of small earthquakes every year, most of which aren't felt. The fault triggers a massive quake once every 400 years or so.* Courtesy of the Utah Geological Survey

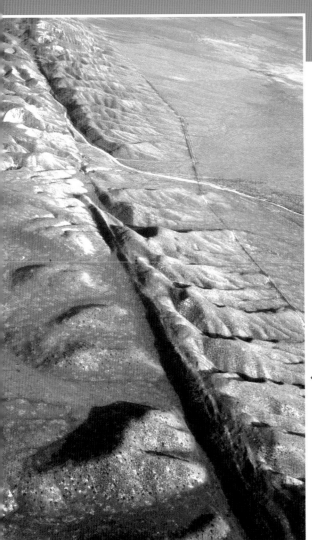

Earthquakes like the one that happened in Erzincan, Turkey, in 1992 can cause damage in just seconds. Clean-up efforts can be complicated by aftershocks – smaller earthquakes that sometimes happen as the rocks along the fault line settle back into place. The '92 Turkish quake had more than 3,000 aftershocks, though many were very small.
© University Corporation for Atmospheric Research (Charles Meertens)

◀ Most faults are underneath the Earth's surface. But the San Andreas fault in California (left), which starts at the California-Mexico border and travels 500 miles (800 km) north to San Francisco, is visible on the ground. It is a major cause of the 10,000 earthquakes the state gets each year.

Earthquakes are so destructive that seismologists have long tried to figure out a way to predict them. So far they've had little luck. They do know that areas that have had quakes in the past are more likely to get them again. They can also perform tests that indicate whether rocks are under stress or pressure – if they are, a quake may be coming. While storms, winds, and other air phenomena can usually be forecasted, what happens underground is much less predictable. It's true for another phenomenon – a really hot one that you'll read about next.

### Did You Know?

Earthquakes are measured by the Richter Magnitude scale, which was developed in 1935 by Charles Richter. A machine called a seismograph (above, right) measures vibrations in the earth. The stronger the vibration, the bigger the quake. Anything less than 6 is usually not serious. Between 6 and 8 is dangerous, and a quake of about 8 usually causes large amounts of damage and destruction.

The largest earthquake ever recorded happened in Chile in May 1960. It was a 9.5 on the Richter scale. More than 1,600 people were killed. Another 3,000 were injured and 2 million people lost their homes. The earthquake also triggered a massive tsunami.

# VOLCANOES: Earth's Eruptions

**Dissecting a Volcano**

PYROCLASTIC MATERIAL

LAVA

MAGMA

MAGMA CHAMBER

Right now, it's likely that 20 volcanoes are erupting molten rock from the inside of our planet to the surface. Earth has 1,500 active volcanoes that have erupted at least once in the last 200 years. One of them – Stromboli, on an Italian island – has erupted every day, several times an hour, for the last 2,000 years! Some volcanoes are dormant, or "sleeping" – they haven't erupted in the last two centuries, but probably will in the future. Others are extinct – they won't erupt ever again.

Just like earthquakes, volcanoes' power comes from Earth's constantly moving tectonic plates. When two tectonic plates collide, a part of one plate may sink, or subduct, beneath another. Around 40 to 60 miles (60 to 100 km) below the surface, the mantle heat melts part of the sinking plate,

▲ *Steam from Mount Erebus in Antarctica freezes when it hits the air, while heat melts snow on the side of the volcano.*
Courtesy Philip R. Kyle

creating a molten rock called magma. This magma is lighter than solid rock and it contains water and carbon dioxide, which makes it bubble upward through the crust like a thick, hot soda pop. This rising magma eventually settles around one to four miles (two to six km) beneath the Earth's surface in underground pools called magma chambers. Like the inside of an unopened soda bottle, the pressure inside these magma chambers is high. When the pressure grows enough, it can crack the rock of the crust, giving the magma a path to the outside in the same way that soda rushes out of a shaken bottle after it's opened.

### Did You Know?
Some scientists think hot, gassy volcanoes could cause global cooling. They say if a volcano spewed enough ash and rock into the stratosphere, it would circulate around the planet and darken the skies. Less sunlight would reach Earth's surface and temperatures would drop.

Some scientists even think volcanic activity led to the extinction of dinosaurs 65 million years ago. They claim that thousands of volcanoes erupted for half a million years, turning the skies black and causing plants to die. Plant-eating dinosaurs died, and the meat-eating dinosaurs (who dined on the plant-eaters) followed.

▲ *Hawaii's Mount Kilauea (above) has been erupting since 1983 and is one of the world's most active volcanoes.*

## Phenomenal Facts

In 1883, a volcano erupted on the Indonesian island of Krakatau in an explosion 13,000 times stronger than an atomic bomb. People heard the boom as far away as Thailand and Australia. This was one of the largest eruptions ever in Indonesia, which is made up of 17,500 islands and has more than 100 active volcanoes.

Indonesia is part of a massive subduction zone in the Pacific Ocean that is loaded with tectonic activity. This "Ring of Fire," as it's called, stretches 25,000 miles (40,000 km), a distance longer than 72,000 CN Towers lined up end to end. The Ring of Fire rumbles with earthquakes and is home to 300 active volcanoes.

Subduction isn't the only way magma reaches Earth. Sometimes plates move apart, creating an opening that allows magma deep underground to bubble to the surface. Magma doesn't even need plates to collide or move apart. In particularly hot areas of the crust called "hotspots," magma bubbles to the surface through openings called plumes. Once magma reaches Earth's surface, it is called lava.

We usually hear about volcanoes that are located on land, but did you know they can also form at the bottom of the ocean? Now let's explore the underwater world - from these raging volcanoes to monster waves.

*A landslide of ash and hot rock (pyroclastic flow) is impossible to outrun: It races downward at 60 miles per hour (97 kph), the same speed as a car on an expressway. If a volcano is especially steep, it goes faster. The avalanche of ash that fell down Mount St. Helens (below) in 1980 reached 300 miles per hour (483 kph).* © University Corporation for Atmospheric Research (Lester Zinser)

*Lava, seen here, is fire hot – 2,000° F (1,100° C), or about 20 times the heat of bathwater. It is hot enough to make a penny shrivel into nothing, and it is very thick and moves very slowly. Over time, a constant flow of lava that cools on the surface is what builds up into the mountain-like shapes.* ▽

### Did You Know?

The Volcanic Explosivity Index ranks eruptions on a scale of 0 to 8. It measures factors such as how often a volcano erupts, how much lava and pyroclastic flow it gives off, and how high that material shoots into the air. An eruption 2.1 million years ago by an extra-powerful "supervolcano" located on the land now known today as Yellowstone National Park was an 8. (Supervolcanoes can produce the largest types of eruptions.)

25

## Nature's Phenomenal Fuel

### Global Warming

Many scientists believe that the patterns ocean water follows as it circulates around the planet is changing due to global warming. But showing exactly how, and explaining what it will mean, may take decades of research. In a search for these answers, scientists have placed buoys and other equipment in ocean water around the world. All sorts of information is collected: how fast the water is moving, in what direction it is traveling, how deep it is flowing, and so on.

Some scientists think that global warming is indeed changing the speed and direction of ocean currents, especially the speed and direction in which cold water sinks to the bottom, then rises and warms. They think changes to these patterns will affect weather all over the planet.

Deep beneath the surface of the ocean, a volcano could be erupting. An earthquake could be shaking. Or, above the water, hot and cold air could be clashing in the atmosphere, forming a storm. When these things happen, the otherwise calm blue ocean thrashes like ice cream in a blender. Gentle waves become gigantic. The water turns wild.

Here's the good news: Earth has an enormous amount of water – three-fourths of the planet is covered by it. So even when a quake shakes, a volcano erupts, or a storm forms, only a portion of the Earth's ocean is directly affected. The results can be deadly in that region, but most of the ocean continues to flow like normal.

Before diving into the details of tsunamis and other deadly waves, let's take a look at how the ocean "normally" works:

Ocean water flows in gigantic rivers called currents. These currents start at the equator, where the sun warms the water to about 80° F (27° C) or higher. Like air in the atmosphere, the warm water moves northward and southward, growing colder as it travels. The same water that was hot enough to power a hurricane off the coast of Florida may only fuel a thunderstorm by the time it reaches New York City. By the time that same water reaches the artic regions of the Earth, it is freezing cold. Near the North and South Poles, this cold water sinks to the bottom of the ocean, where it creeps back toward the equator and eventually warms up again. This part of the process is *really* slow – the water can take 500 years to travel the length of North America.

*Global warming is causing glaciers like this one to melt, increasing the amount of water in the oceans. Since water is the fuel for thunderstorms and hurricanes, some scientists caution that having more of it could make these storms even stronger in the future.*

## Did You Know?

Tides can trigger earthquakes underwater. Scientists learned this by placing seismometers (to measure earthquakes) and tilt-meters (to measure tides) on an underwater Pacific Ocean volcano a few hundred miles off the coast of Oregon. In two months, more than 400 small earthquakes were recorded, mostly during low tide. Scientists figured out that less water put less weight on the faults, which made it easier for them to slip and cause quakes. High tide, on the other hand, pressed down on the faults and mostly pinned them in place.

The Loop Current (above) is a river-like flow of water that starts in the Caribbean Sea, travels around Cuba, and curves through the Gulf of Mexico. It's warm (79° F/26° C) and deep (300 feet/91 meters, the length of a football field). Scientists keep track of it because the Loop Current and its eddies (as seen at right) – small, spinning currents that form on its sides – provide the perfect fuel for strong hurricanes.

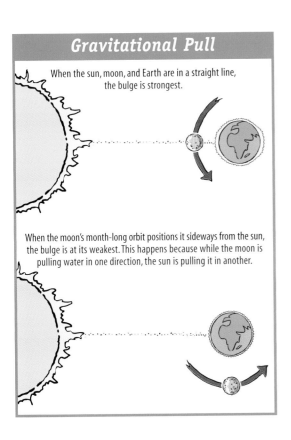

## Gravitational Pull

When the sun, moon, and Earth are in a straight line, the bulge is strongest.

When the moon's month-long orbit positions it sideways from the sun, the bulge is at its weakest. This happens because while the moon is pulling water in one direction, the sun is pulling it in another.

The winds that blow across the ocean push currents with them. You can see this effect easily: the waves that wash ashore on a beach are caused by the wind. What you can't see without a satellite is that Earth's rotation makes the wind (and the water) curve, creating big loopy currents.

The sun works with the moon to affect the flow of Earth's water in another way. Each has a gravitational pull that "yanks" on the ocean, causing the water to move in a tidal wave. When the sun, moon, and Earth are in a straight line, water bunches up, or bulges, on the side of the Earth that is closest to the moon. A second bulge of water that didn't get pulled forms on the opposite side of the planet. As the Earth rotates, different areas pass through the "bulge" (see diagram at left). The bulge, where the water is deepest, is known as "high tide." The thinnest part of the water, meanwhile, is "low tide."

Understanding ocean currents fully is complicated. That's the job of oceanographers – people who study tides, winds, and more to make predictions about the ocean. But even for these highly skilled scientists, the water is full of surprises – like the killer waves that strike with little or no warning.

# Tsunamis: Earth's Mighty Waves

Picture a peaceful harbor. People are strolling along the shoreline. The sun shines on the glistening blue water. Fishermen are casting for a big catch from boats floating gently off the shore. Suddenly, cell phones start buzzing with text messages. Radios are chirping with alarm signals. People need to get out of the water and away from the shore – now! A giant wave will hit in only half an hour.

This is a warning for a tsunami (SOO-nahm-ee), the Japanese word for "harbor wave." Tsunamis are a series of massive waves that begin deep in the ocean, travel seven times faster than a cheetah can run, and reach as high as a two-floor shopping mall. They temporarily disrupt the ocean's regular patterns of currents by creating a wall of waves that crashes ashore with a roar.

Tsunamis hit land most often in places located around the Ring of Fire: Japan, Russia, Alaska, the Philippines, and Central and South America.

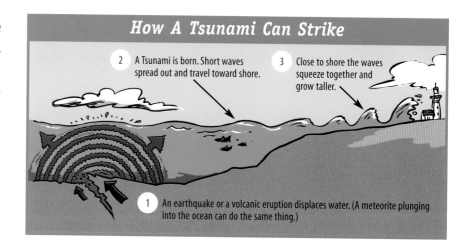

### How A Tsunami Can Strike

**2** A Tsunami is born. Short waves spread out and travel toward shore.

**3** Close to shore the waves squeeze together and grow taller.

**1** An earthquake or a volcanic eruption displaces water. (A meteorite plunging into the ocean can do the same thing.)

*Notice how the water is relatively thin at the bottom of this tsunami wave? That's because as the tsunami reaches land, it pulls water back from the shore and shifts it into the top, or crest, of the wave.* ▼

## Phenomenal Facts

For hundreds of years, sailors spoke of monster waves that sank ships. But nobody could ever prove these "rogue" (or "unpredictable") waves existed until last century, when radio equipment and other technology helped prove that, yes, gigantic waves sometimes do come out of nowhere. In 2005, a cruise ship off the Florida coast was flooded by one. In 1978, a German tanker the size of two and a half soccer fields was sunk by one in the middle of the Atlantic Ocean.

Scientists using satellites have discovered that rogue waves can double the height of a typical large wave and reach 90 feet (27 meters), or as tall as a 10-story building. But the cause of rogue waves remains a mystery to this day.

**TSUNAMI HAZARD ZONE**

**IN CASE OF EARTHQUAKE GO TO HIGH GROUND OR INLAND**

As you know, earthquakes and volcanic eruptions occur under the water – or even near it, in the case of the Krakatau volcano you read about on page 25 – just like they do on land, and cause large amounts of water to be moved, or displaced. This creates a series of very long waves that, at first, can barely be seen. In the middle of the ocean, the waves will be about three feet (one meter) tall. People on ships may not even notice the wave. But scientists who use satellites to monitor these kinds of waves will notice ... and

▲ In December 2004, a tsunami caused by a 9.3 earthquake under the Indian Ocean killed more than 300,000 people and destroyed entire communities.

will watch carefully. As the waves get closer to shore, they will squeeze together, grow taller, and travel faster. Tsunami waves can hit 500 mph (800 kph) and regularly reach 100 feet (30 meters) tall or more. The highest tsunami ever hit Japan in 1971. It was 278 feet (85 meters) – that's nearly the length of a football field.

Ring of Fire lands like Japan aren't the only ones at risk. Tsunamis can strike anywhere located near a large body of water. Plus, there's another way a tsunami can start. If a large **meteorite** from outer space were to plunge into the ocean, tons of water would be displaced – and a massive tsunami would rush toward shore.

The state of Hawaii and some countries located in the Ring of Fire have warning systems so when scientists detect a tsunami, people can be alerted quickly. Speed is key, because a tsunami is deadly and offers no more warning than a few hours – and, often, less.

### Global Warming

Coral reefs (as seen at right) are a barrier to waves and can help protect people and land from tsunamis. But the rising sea levels that result from melting glaciers are bad news for these reefs. Deeper water means the reefs won't get enough sunlight. When this happens, they die. Likewise, reefs can be damaged or killed by even a slight increase in ocean-water temperature.

When nature's forces align, our planet flexes its muscles. The resulting phenomena may *look* spectacular, but they're often destructive – and even deadly. You can't stop the devastation, but you do have the power to help our planet – and the people on it – in many ways:

1. You can help people who have been affected by the disasters these phenomena cause. Relief organizations send food, clothing, medicine, and tents for shelter, among other materials, to aid both the disaster victims and the people trying to help them. You can help from home by raising money or collecting clothing or equipment to donate. Try ideas such as:

- Organizing a bake sale to raise money for a relief organization.
- Working with your school to hold an event for which ticket sales benefit people in a disaster-struck region.
- Holding a clothing or canned-goods drive to help people who have lost their homes.

▲ *When a series of tornadoes raged through the southern and midwestern United States in May 2008, more than two dozen people were killed and thousands of homes and buildings were destroyed (as seen above). That same month, China was rattled by an earthquake that measured 7.9 on the Richter scale and lasted a whopping three minutes. The devastation was massive: One week afterward, at least 70,000 people were known to be dead or missing. Just days before this quake, a cyclone stormed through the country of Burma (also known as Myanmar), killing 78,000 people and leaving hundreds of thousands more homeless.* FEMA/Barry Bahler

Try coming up with your own ideas too. Be sure to work with an adult who can assist you with the details and get you in touch with an organization that can use your help.

2. You can talk to others about global warming. As you know, global warming is caused by the amount of $CO_2$ in the atmosphere. We've put a lot of it there ourselves. While we can't simply take it out, we can prepare for the changes it is bringing ... and we can stop putting so much $CO_2$ into the air. Around the world, kids are organizing recycling drives, water-saving days, and other Earth-friendly activities. Some kids have even created web sites and speeches designed to spread the word. You can do something, too, even if it's as simple as creating a poster to hang in your school, or writing a letter to elected officials, asking them to create laws that promote recycling and cut down on pollution.

# Answer: *Very* – in ways we're still discovering.

*On this mountain trail, signs tell visitors what phenomena to look for at different times of the year.* ▶
© University Corporation for Atmospheric Research

Other things you can do are:

- Talk to your family and have an emergency plan. If a storm hits, where is the safest place to go? Who can you call on for help? What supplies should you have in the house?
- Remember the three *R*s: Reduce, Reuse, Recycle. One of the biggest reasons so much CO2 is in the atmosphere is that we're cutting down entire forests of trees to make paper and wood products. You can help decrease the need by borrowing books and magazines from the library. When you're done with ones you own, donate them to your library. You can also encourage your family to recycle boxes and newspapers along with cans and bottles, and so on. See what steps you can take every day to make the three *R*s a habit.
- Walk, run ... have fun outdoors. If you can safely walk or ride a bike, scooter, or skateboard somewhere instead of asking someone to drive you, do it.

3. Become a scientist. In this book you read about the action in the air, on the land, and in the water. Which was most interesting? If you liked learning about what happens in the air, maybe you're a meteorologist in the making. If you preferred getting the scoop on land, you might be a future seismologist or volcanologist. Or maybe the water action splashed your imagination. If so, you could be a future oceanographer. You can get started *now* by researching the phenomena that interest you most. In fact, you're sure to learn about even more phenomena that aren't packed into these pages.

So, you can't control our powerful planet, but you *can* make a positive impact.

- You *can* assist people affected by disaster.
- You *can* do something to fight global warming.
- And you *can* become a scientist who may solve one of the many natural mysteries someday.

If you take action, you'll help our planet Earth – and the people on it. That's the power *you* have!

*This student studies a water sample from a wetland – an area of land set aside where plants and animals can grow and live safely.*
© University Corporation for Atmospheric Research

◀ *Some museums can help you get up close with phenomena that are dangerous in the real world. This student uses a contraption to learn about microbursts – strong and sudden downward winds.*
© University Corporation for Atmospheric Research

**Avalanche:** Heavy amounts of snow and ice that tumble down a mountain slope.

**Celsius:** a system of numbers for measuring temperatures, used in Canada and most other countries. It was created in 1742 by Swedish scientist Anders Celsius.

**Climate:** the weather in a place over a period of time.

**Condensation:** when water cools and collects in droplets.

**Drought:** a long period of time with little to no rain.

**El Niño:** The appearance of especially warm water every three to six years in the western part of the Pacific Ocean; it kills fish and changes weather around the planet.

▲ *Land in areas affected by drought gets dry and cracked, like chapped skin.*

**Equator:** an invisible line on the Earth that is halfway between the North Pole and the South Pole. It divides the Earth's northern part, or hemisphere, from its southern hemisphere.

**Fahrenheit:** a system of numbers for measuring temperatures, used in the United States. It is named after its German creator, Daniel Gabriel Fahrenheit, who introduced it in 1724.

**Gravity:** forces that pull objects toward the center of Earth. The moon and sun have gravity too.

**Meteorologist:** a scientist who studies the atmosphere to predict weather.

**Oceanographer:** a scientist who studies ocean currents and water phenomena.

**Precipitation:** rain, snow, sleet, hail, and other forms of weather that fall from the sky.

**Radar:** equipment that uses invisible waves to measure the size and direction of storms.

▲ *A computer-made image of a satellite orbiting Earth.*

**Satellite:** a human-made object that orbits around Earth and gathers useful information through photographs and radar.

**Seismologist:** a scientist who studies earthquakes.

**Storm surge:** large waves of water that crash onto land and often cause floods.

**Temperature:** the degree of hotness or coldness of the air, measured in Fahrenheit or Celsius.

**Volcanologist:** a scientist who studies volcanoes.

**Weather:** conditions in the atmosphere on a specific day, including both temperature and precipitation.

▼ *A storm surge crashes ashore.*